A Pondering Soul

Konner Ninh

Presentation by *BookLeaf Publishing*

Web: www.bookleafpub.com

E-mail: info@bookleafpub.com

ISBN: 9789357746724

First edition 2022

First love

When I first saw you
I realized that I was not alone
My emotions express my love for you
The love I give you is to be shown

When I am lost in the darkest night
I think of you as my brightest light
If you give me this second chance
I will cherish every moment with you
Can I please have this dance?

A true reflection

I see myself in the mirror
My life an endless thriller
Everything much clearer
Escaping the terror

A reflection of my life
A roller coaster never-ending
A reflection of my heart
My love never bending

My mirror broke into shards
Glass on the floor
Playing my cards
To end the war

At the waters
My reflection is clear
Counting the quarters
My true self is here

My leeching light

Deep down under
We are always alone
I may enjoy your light
But I am my own way home

Below the surface
I am number one
Your light shines through
But I make my own fun

Beyond the skin
I am a cave
Your light starts to fade
But I bury my own grave

Far up above
We are always together
I may enjoy your light
But I am my own weather

A great escape

Folding my clothes
Packing my things
Plucking the strings
Of the puppet's soul

My tears are dripping
Soaking the paper
The ink is smearing
The colors are fading

Writing the letter
With no regret
Worse but better
Watching the sunset

Free and alive
A night with no home
Trying to survive
The streets on my own

Pure love

Love is a reminder
Of who you fight for
The feeling where
Pure love is never a blur

Listen to the sound
Of your beating heart
The place where
Pure love will be found

A true vision coming alive
To closely listen is where
Pure love will thrive

Trust flooding my thoughts
Of your intelligent mind
The stairs where
Pure love is your climb

A story rewritten

Never be afraid to break
the mold that you
were forced to fake.
Your story begins now

This is your story
that keeps unfolding daily.
So why not choose
to write it bravely

Bravery is there
residing within your chest.
A gift your heart shares
with your mind and the rest

Bits and pieces
are falling into place.
Making a story
of compassion and grace

The scenic route

I am the waves of my ocean
washing over my pain
I am a leaf on my tree
dancing in the rain

I am the sand at the beach
filled with seashells
I am the melodious speech
filled with whistles and bells

I am the roar of a lion,
big and bold
I am a temple
made of silver and gold

The gas in the light

Overused excuses
to make me stay
Blowing my fuses
to aid my dismay

Useless reasons
Delaying my growth
Endless seasons
Making me loath

A worthless memory
thrown in my face
A triumphant story
to finish the race

Unwanted feelings
consuming my heart
Pointless kneeling
worshiping the worst part

An empty life

Empty lots and streets
Nothing but silence
Just an empty feast
With no one at the table

No street lights
Nothing but darkness
My space race to Mars
is blasting without me in the front seat

No candles to light
No battles to fight
Just an empty victory
To relive the glory

No mail in the box
No packages at the door
Just piles of broken seashells
Filling the shore

Holidays reimagined

I fall in love again
Every Valentine's Day
Forever falling for you
In a whole new way

No teddy bears
No boxes of chocolate
Rides at county fairs
And building a rocket

I fall in love again
Every Christmas
Opening gifts
And drinking champagne

No glistening lights
Wrapped around the tree
Beautiful sights
Watching the sea

Love in the chaos

We both thought
Our love was chaos
so we separated,
just to only realize
it made it worse

Where is the trust
in this so-called chaos
Love turning into dust

We both ought
to come back to the chaos
that once separated us
just to breathe in
the smoke from the same fire

The love is still there
Yet it feels like
My heart is sheared
by the love that feels so true it's feared

Silver-lining

They tell me
Not all love
is supposed to hurt

They tell me
A rose has more petals
than thorns

They tell me
A book has more pages
than words

They tell me
A balloon has more air
than rubber

I have been told
So many things about love
It is full of heartbreak
All I have to do is be bold

Internal strength

No matter how strong
A person may appear
You will never know
What is truly going on
Even if it may seem clear

I keep a smile
To hide all the pain
To cover up our scars
But my strength comes from
The size of my heart
And the dream of my stars

To keep an open mind
Is a task within itself
But soon I will find
The strength to be kind

A changed universe

The universe is trying
to come through to you;
Will you listen, too?

My ears are tainted
by the society we live in.
How will I listen
if all they care about
is where I failed again?

My ears are clogged
by the people who think
I am weak on my own.
How will I listen
if all they care about
is when I am alone?

The universe has been answered
I have come through
by listening to the sounds calling to me.

Joyous seasons

How you feel is the reason
For what comes next
How you feel each season
Is what lies ahead

Summer thrills
Endless smiles
Winter chills
Endless snow piles

Autumn leaves
changing colors
Spring bees
And vibrant colors

Each season
feeling so similar
Each reason
feeling so sure

Me time

It took me a while
to realize
that it is okay
to say no
it is okay
to choose yourself

It is not selfish
to believe in self-love
It is not cruel
to rise above

It took me a while
to learn
that it is okay
to take deep breaths
it is okay
to take a step back
to get back on track

My fairytale

No, the sparkle in her eyes
That got me entwined
Not even her sweet embrace
But her brilliant mind

Her beautiful words
is a calming balm to my mind
Her strong action
such a joyful ride

Not the shine in her hair
that got me entranced
Not even her hugs and kisses
But her elegant dance

Her beautiful moves
are sweeping my floor
Her strong footwork
makes me ready to soar

My solar system

Love is the gravity
that pulls me toward you
I travel at high speeds
to find you

My moons orbit your planet
I never lose my course
I never lose my path
My path to stay with you

You are the star
that sparkles in the night
that opens my eyes
to an elegant and beautiful sight

I rise

Worlds are crashing down on me
Times are fading out with me
Clouds are crying, now I'm free
From a seed to a growing tree

I stand here
Weak, alone
In the corner on my own
Defeated
With my mind so still
Thoughts turned into fears
Dreams into tears

Drowning in the seas of lies
The truth will let me rise
Looking for myself once more
My wings are ready to soar

I stand here
Looking to the sky
With the moon
And the stars aligned
From the shadows of the cave
I am the light that lights the way

My world is never what it used to be

The clock reached its end
The clouds sing in glee
From an enemy to a friend

I am who I am

In my pupils, fire blazing
Burning the trees of my soul
And turning my body into ash
Blowing away in the wind
Spreading across the soil of my spirit

My heart falls into the ocean of despair
Washing away the compassion in my heart
Polluting the rivers of my forgiveness
Infecting the watershed of my sincerity

The birds of my hopes and dreams
Laying dead on the soil that I have buried my
sorrows
The bears of my kindness and optimism
Covered in the ashes of my soul
The fishes of my motivation
Suffocating in the lake of my hatred

Hurdling over the mountain of change
Is a journey I have to take alone
Constantly bumping to the rocks of judgment
Being crushed by the rockslide of my demise

In my hair, the rainbow shines
Changes the pen I used to write my own destiny

From black to blue
My parents view me differently
As if the child they raised is not there anymore
As if the innocence I had is lost
As if the confidence I gained is lost
As if the resilience I developed is lost
I am who I am

A mindful storm

I can hear
the thunder in my heart
I can see
the lightning in my eyes

Filled with rain
pouring all my hatred
taking away the pain
Of the love I once gated

I can feel
the fire of my soul
I can touch
the flowers of my goal

All my senses
Coming alive
breaking down my fences
Before I arrive